# Animals

Written by Nina Filipek
Illustrations by Jeannette O'Toole

Can you see:

# In the jungle!

Look who's hiding in the jungle. Who's got stripes?

monkey

snake

 **Learning Together**

- Learn the names of the animals in the scene.
- Talk about each animal.
- Make an animal scrapbook with your own drawings and photos cut from magazines.

Can you see:

# In the ocean!

Look who's swimming in the ocean.
Who's the scary one?

whale

shark

### Learning Together

- Discuss the differences between animals that live on land and animals that live in the sea.
- Make an ocean picture. Draw some ocean creatures in wax crayon and then apply a blue colour wash over the top.
- Think of some animals that begin with the same letter as your child's name.

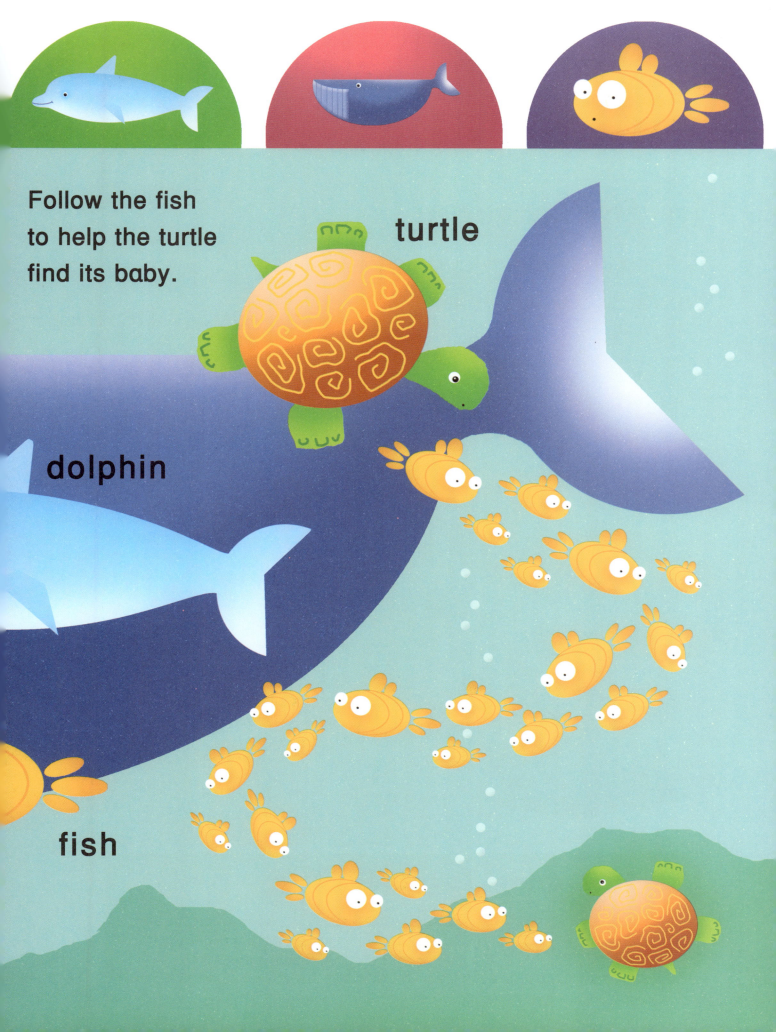

Can you see:

# In the ice!

Who's bathing in the icy water?
Who's just caught a fish?

polar bear

seal

 **Learning Together**

- Discuss what the weather would be like in the Arctic.
- Talk about how the animals that live there protect themselves from the cold.
- Point to where the Arctic is on a globe.

Can you see:

# In the outback!

Colour the parrots so they look the same.

parrots

alligator

## Learning Together

- Tell your child that a baby kangaroo is called a 'joey'. Talk about how the joey stays in its mother's pouch until it can look after itself.
- Find out as much as you can about Australia and its unique animals.

Can you see:

# In the grasslands!

Who grazes in the grasslands?
Who's the tallest?

giraffe

lion

 **Learning Together**

- Point out that the giraffe is the tallest animal and that the ostrich the fastest bird on land.
- Look at the pattern on the giraffe and the zebra's skin.
- If you've seen these animals at a zoo or wildlife park, recall your visit.

## Can you see:

# In the sky!

The eagle has hidden its nest in the rocks. Can you spot it?

seagull

eagle

### Learning Together

- Introduce your child to the word 'nocturnal' and help them decide which of these animals it applies to.
- Point out that all the animals in this scene, apart from the bat, are birds.
- Make a collage picture of a bird using coloured card and feathers.

bats

Who's not afraid of flying in the dark?

woodpecker

owl

Can you see:

# By the lake!

dragonfly

swan

frog

### Learning Together

- Discuss the differences between birds and other animals.
- Talk about animal life cycles, e.g. from tadpole to frog, and from egg to duck.
- Introduce your child to the words: gosling, duckling, cygnet.

Can you see:

# On the farm!

Who lives on the farm?

chick

calf

pig

sheep

### Learning Together

- Talk about each of the farm animals in the picture.
- Ask questions, e.g. which animal lays eggs? Which animal gives us wool?
- Plan a visit to a farm, or recall a recent visit.

Match the babies with their mothers.
Learn the babies' names.

chicken

cow

piglet

lamb

Can you see:

# In the garden!

Look who's in the garden.

butterfly

bee

Which animals like the flowers in the garden?

##  Learning Together

- Talk about the life cycle of the butterfly. Read Eric Carle's The Hungry Caterpillar.
- Look for other animals that live in the garden, e.g. worms, ladybirds and birds.

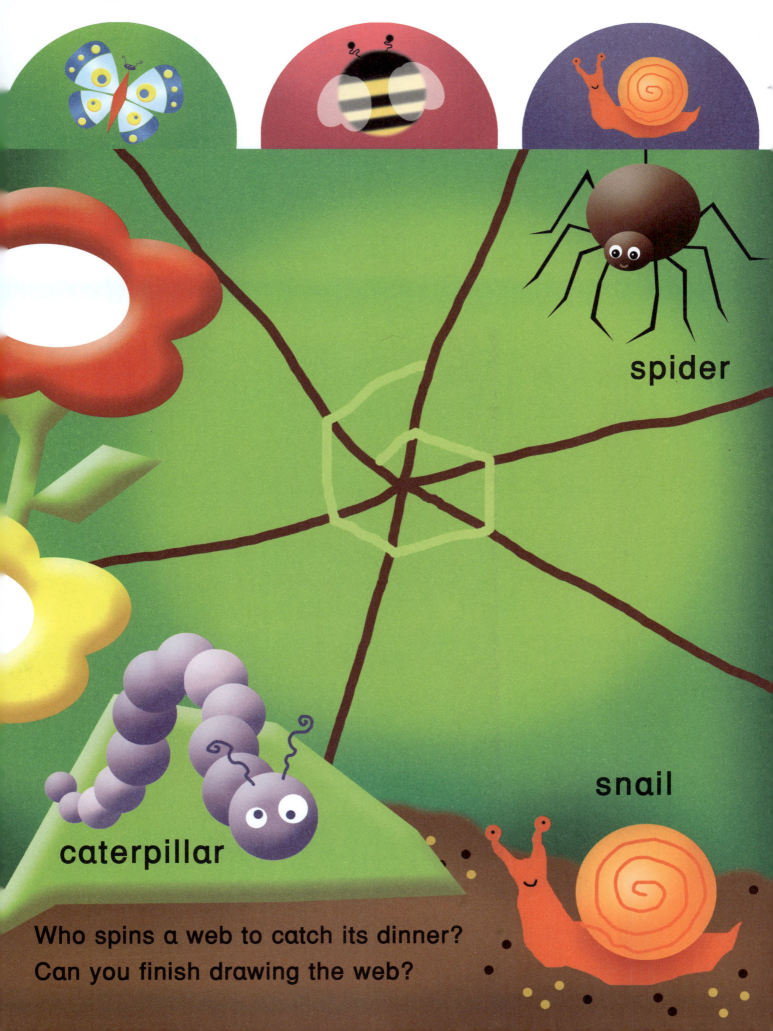

Can you see:

# At home!

Do any of these animals live at home with you?

stable

kennel

dog

hutch

cat

 **Learning Together**

- Talk about animals that make good pets.
- Discuss how pets should be cared for and looked after.
- Learn to read some simple animal names, e.g. cat, dog, rabbit.

# Snail trail!

Follow the snail trail and colour in the animals you pass on the way. Which is your favourite?

## Learning Together

- Draw spirals and turn them into drawings of snails.
- Learn to draw your favourite animal.
- Look for non-fiction books about animals in the library.